Christmas

Program Builder
No. 59

LILLENAS®
DRAMA

Christmas

Program Builder
No. 59

Creative
Resources
for Program
Directors

Compiled by **Kim Messer**

Lillenas PUBLISHING COMPANY

KANSAS CITY, MO 64141

Questions? Please write or call:
    Lillenas Publishing Company
    Drama Resources
    P.O. Box 419527
    Kansas City, MO 64141
    Phone: 816-931-1900 • Fax: 816-412-8390
    E-mail: drama@lillenas.com
    Web Site: www.lillenasdrama.com

Cover design by: Mike Walsh

Contents

Contents

Preschool Recitations

Mary Said

Mary said, "I carry God's Son,
Baby Jesus, the Holy One."

Mary Ann Green

What I Like to Say

Once more it's time to tell you
    What I always like to say,
"I wish you a Merry Christmas
    And a happy New Year's Day."

Margaret Primrose

Child

He was a child when He came.
Jesus was His Holy name.

Mary Ann Green

I Wonder

CHILD 1: What was it like in the
            stable
          Where the Baby Jesus
            lay?
CHILD 2: Was it cold and dark and
            smelly?
          Did He sleep on
            scratchy hay?
CHILD 3: Did a donkey complain
            with a hee-haw
          That was joined by a
            mournful moo?
CHILD 4: Did a sparrow flit and
            flutter
          Or just nod his head
            and coo?
CHILD 5: Were there spiders and
            scurrying mice
          In that lowly cattle
            shed?
CHILD 6: Did the animals nibble
            the hay
          That served as Jesus'
            bed?
CHILD 1: I'd have liked to watch
            His mother
          As she wrapped Him in
            swaddling clothes.
CHILD 2: I wonder if she hugged
            Him
          And felt His fingers
            and toes.
CHILD 3: What was it like for Jesus
          To leave His home in
            the sky
CHILD 4: And come to this wicked
            old world
          To suffer, and bleed,
            and die?
CHILD 5: Though I don't know the
            answers,
          I know it was a
            wonderful night
CHILD 6: When Jesus came from
            heaven
          To make our lives
            happy and bright.

Margaret Primrose

Christmas Riddles

ALL:
We have a game
We want to share with
you.
Each letter that we hold
Will give you a clue.

CLUE 1 *(holding letter "A"; two or more children in unison):*
We're a multitude
Who winged our way to
earth.
We sang to lowly
shepherds
The night of Jesus' birth.
Who are we? (Angels)

CLUE 2 *(holding letter "S"; two or more boys in unison):*
We were frightened by
the angels,
But soon were filled with
joy.
We heard about a
Savior—
A newborn baby boy.
Who are we? (Shepherds)

CLUE 3 *(holding letter "M"; one girl):*
I'm the peasant mother
Of the newborn King of
kings.
Thank God for the Child
And the joy He brings.
Who am I? (Mary)

CLUE 4 *(holding letter "C"; one small child):*
I am the Baby
Who slept in a manger.
I was taken to Egypt
To protect Me from
danger.
Who am I? (the Christ
child)

CLUE 5 *(holding letter "S"; one voice):*
Some wise men from the
east
Saw my great shining light.
They rested while I hid
And followed me by night.
What am I? (Star)

CLUE 6 *(holding letter "I"; one voice):*
I'm one of the gifts
The wise men gave away
To a babe in Bethlehem
Who slept on the hay.
What am I? (Incense)

CLUE 7 *(holding letters "R" and "T"; two voices):*
Can you give us other
words
For silver and gold?
Their beginning letters
Are the ones we hold.
What are we? (Riches and
Treasures)

CLUE 8 *(holding letter "H"; one voice):*
He is the ruler
Whose plot was to kill.
He didn't succeed.
It wasn't God's will.
Who was he? (Herod)

ALL:
What word can you make
With the letters that you
see?
If you know, help us
shout it
When we count to three.
One, two, three.

(Children holding letters step forward and form the word)

CHRISTMAS

Margaret Primrose

Happy Bells

(CHILD *may ring a bell while reciting*)
Listen to the happy bells
Ringing loud and clear,
So that everyone will know
Christmas time is here.

Robert Colbert

Christmas Day

Christmas Day! Christmas Day!
We are happy so we say,
Merry Christmas! Merry
    Christmas!
What a happy, happy day!

Debbie Salter Goodwin

In the Stall

Baby Jesus in the stall
Came because He loved us all.

Mary Ann Green

Ages 5 to 7

WHO WAS IT?

(TEACHER asks the questions, showing pictures to prompt CHILDREN to answer with two-line rhyme.)

TEACHER *(picture of Mary and Joseph):* Who had to go to Bethlehem because the King said so?

> CHILDREN: Mary and Joseph went to Bethlehem.
> It was a long, long way to go.

TEACHER *(picture of Mary on a donkey):* Who carried Mary carefully and never let her fall?

> CHILDREN: The donkey carried Mary
> And did not trip at all. *(Shaking heads "no")*

TEACHER *(picture of innkeeper):* Who sent them to a stable where all the animals stay?

> CHILDREN: The innkeeper sent them to the stable
> Where they had to sleep on hay. *(Resting heads on clasped hands)*

TEACHER *(picture of shepherds on hillside):* Who were on the hillside watching sheep by night?

> CHILDREN: The shepherds were on the hillside
> When they saw a very great light. *(Hide eyes as if from light)*

TEACHER *(picture of wise men):* Who came with gifts for the Baby? Who came from very far?

> CHILDREN: The wise men came to Jesus
> By following a very bright star. *(Point to sky)*

TEACHER *(picture of Jesus):* Who came from God to give us love? How can we celebrate that special day?

> CHILDREN: Jesus came from God to say,
> "I came to give my love away." *(Right hands over heart, then thrust out in a give-away gesture)*

Debbie Salter Goodwin

Bells of Joy

Joy bells are ringing out
To celebrate Jesus' birth.
In wonder we pause to remember
The blessings He brought to earth.

Dorothy Heibel

Salvation's Light

CHILD 1: Christ is born,
New hope He brings.
Hail Him Lord
And mighty King.

CHILD 2: Love and joy
Come down to earth
At the Savior's
Holy birth.

CHILD 3: He has brought
Salvation's light,
God's great gift
And glory bright.

CHILD 4: Bless and praise Him,
Worship Him too.
Christ is God's proof
His word is true.

CHILD 5: Come, be thankful,
Behold, be thrilled,
The miracle of Christmas
Is Jesus, for real.

Robert Colbert

We Did Our Part

(Each CHILD *should be in character costume if possible.)*

CHILD 1: I am the star
That led the way
To the house where Jesus
The Christ child lay.

CHILD 2: I'm one of the angels
Who came to earth.
That long ago night
When we announced
Jesus' birth.

CHILD 3: I am the innkeeper
Who had only a stall
To offer the Savior
Of one and all.

CHILD 4: My name is Joseph;
Mary is my wife.
God chose me to shelter
The Giver of eternal life.

CHILD 5: I was only a peasant,
But I was the one
God chose as the mother
Of His only begotten Son.

CHILD 6: I'm one of the shepherds
Who heard the angels sing.
"Glory in the highest
To the newborn King."

CHILD 7: I'm one of the kings
Who came from afar.
We found Baby Jesus
By following a star.

ALL: We all had a part
In the Christmas story.
Thanks be to God.
We give Him the glory.

Margaret Primrose

Each Heart

May the peace of God
Enter each heart
As we worship and praise
Our newborn Lord.
Merry Christmas

Robert Colbert

I Know

Yes, I know
A star shone bright,
I know that angels sang.
I know a little King was born,
And Jesus was His name.

Robert Colbert

Shepherds

Shepherds followed the star
But they didn't go too far.
They found the Child on the hay
That very first Christmas Day.
They knelt before the little One
And worshiped Him, God's only Son.

Mary Ann Green

God's Christmas Gift

God's gift of the Holy Jesus
Was given to man in love,
That we would turn away from sin
And worship the Father above.

Dorothy Heibel

Angels Sing

Listen to those hymns of joy
The angel choir sings!
Praising the birth of Jesus,
Lord of lords and King of kings!

Dorothy Heibel

Rejoice! Rejoice!

Hooray! Hooray!
It's Christmas morn.
Give a mighty shout!
Rejoice! Rejoice!
Christ is born.
That's what it's all about.

Robert Colbert

I Wish I'd Been

(A few costume items and simple props add interest. Each CHILD *should freeze after delivering their line until the last stanza.)*

CHILD 1 *(with a stamped letter):*
> I wish I'd been Augustus,
> That census bureau guy.
> I would have made exceptions
> And let Joseph use e-mail reply.

CHILD 2 *(with pillow):*
> I wish I'd been a traveler
> Beside the donkey's stride.
> I would have shared my pillow
> To give Mary an easy ride.

CHILD 3 *(with broom or tray):*
> I wish I'd been the innkeeper.
> I wouldn't think of saying, "No."
> "Take my room," I would have said,
> "If you have nowhere to go."

CHILD 4: I wish I'd been King Herod.
> I wouldn't have been so mean.
> I would have joined the wise men
> To give my heart to the King. *(kneels and bows)*

(Actors break freeze to say their line or use other children.)

CHILD 1: We all would rewrite the story.

CHILD 2: We prefer an easier way.

CHILD 3: But God used every detail

CHILD 4: To deliver what He wanted to say:

CHILD 1: We think we would have been different.
We think we would have been kind.

CHILD 2: But how do we treat Him in everyday life?
What Jesus-first ways do *you* find?

CHILD 3: So take your place in the story.
Make sure there is room at *your* inn.

CHILD 4: Protect your journey to worship
And you'll never say "I wish I'd been . . ."

Debbie Salter Goodwin

Ages 8 to 10

The Donkey's Tale

Rest, tired donkey, gently rest.
The burden you bore was heaven-
    blest.
Mary, His mother, great with child,
In spite of her labor, sweetly smiled.

Now the Infant you brought us is
    safely here
While cattle and sheep are watching
    near.
His cradle, a manger soft with hay
On this, His wonderful natal day.

So rest, little donkey, your journey
    is done.
The world will know that you were
    the one
Who safely carried a royal King,
While shepherds pray and angels
    sing.

Jean Conder Soule

Let's Welcome

Let's welcome
The little Christ child
Lying upon the hay,
Who brought to us
Salvation's joy
That first Christmas day.

Robert Colbert

The Dove's Lullaby

Turtle dove, in the rafters high,
You sang Him to sleep with a
    lullaby.
You were the first to see His face
Nestled in hay in that humble place.
You were the first who sang the song
That kept Him at peace the whole
    night long.

Jean Conder Soule

Adult Recitations

Whose Idea was *This?*

I stand here in this buffet line,
Waiting for my turn to dine,
Smelling turkey, waiting . . . waiting
All my taste buds salivating . . .
My favorite never was buffet,
Especially not on Christmas day.

At last, at last, my turn has come.
Lovely dinner, yum, yum, yum . . .
All the fixin's taste as good
As I, remembering, knew they would.
If only it weren't true that I
Must soon line up again—for pie.

Florence Boutwell

Little One

Wake up, little one, it is
   Christmas morn.
     The gifts are under the tree.
Rub the sleep from your eyes,
   little one,
     There are new toys to see.
Never forget, little one,
     Why we celebrate this day,
Because of the birth of God's own
   Son
     Who takes all sin away.

Robert E. Snodgrass

The Same Today, Yesterday, and Forever

It's been a while since Christmas
   was
A simple homespun day,
With homemade gifts and home-
   made treats
And Santa on a sleigh;
Since Father cut the Christmas
   tree
And Mother stuffed the bird,
And family carols and hymns in
   church
Were the only music heard;
So long ago . . . no shopping
   malls,
No guests brought in on jets.
No artificial Christmas trees
Nor January debts.
And then last night I saw the
   star—
The heavens seemed aflame;
The only thing that mattered was
The message was the same:
   "Glory to God in the highest
and on earth peace and goodwill
     toward men." Luke 2:14

Florence Boutwell

Sleep, Baby, Sleep

*(Could be delivered by an "angel" or
performed as a reading)*
Sleep, little Baby, soundly sleep
Snug in a manger near cattle and
    sheep.
Mary, Your mother, is watching
    You.
Sleep, dearest Child, so precious and
    new.

A dove in the rafters up above
Will sing You a lullaby of love.
Rest, little Baby, rest till morn
When the world will know the
    Christ child is born.

Then shepherds will come to kneel
    and pray
Beside the rude cradle where in the
    hay
You lie in Your swaddling clothes
    secure—
The Son of God, so gracious and
    pure.

                    Jean Conder Soule

A Different Christmas

The days are passing, Christmas is
    nearing,
Red and green lights are
    reappearing;
Carols are playing in all the malls,
Tinsel decorates town banquet halls.

I'm mailing out greetings, doing all
    that I can
To make Christmas happen
    according to plan,
Aware of an ache no pretending
    erases—
The longing for loved ones in far
    away places.

                    Florence Boutwell

Christmas Plays

ANGELS AMONG US
A Readers Theatre for Angel Sunday
by Mark Morgan

Running Time: 15 to 20 minutes

Theme: Remembering the true meaning of Christmas in our present world

Cast:
> READER 1—ANGEL 1
> READER 2—ANGEL 2
> READER 3—ANGEL 3
> READER 4—MAN/WOMAN

Props:
> Anaheim Angels baseball caps for the angels

Production Note: As a readers theatre, the stage is set with four stools, one for each Reader. At the beginning, the Readers are speaking on-stage as themselves. When the scene changes, the three angels are on the front porch of the Man/Woman's house on Christmas Eve.

READER 1: Angels are everywhere.

READER 2: On bumper stickers.

READER 3: In checkout lines.

READER 4: On television.

READER 1: I don't drive faster than my angels can fly.

READER 3: I saw an angel save my cat.

READER 2: Angels are watching over me.

READER 4: Yes, angels are among us everywhere it seems.

READER 3: But, what would happen . . .

READER 2: If angels,

READER 3: Real angels,

READER 4: Like the ones that appeared in the night sky over Bethlehem,

READER 1: Showed up on our doorstep?

(READERS *change their appearance to show they've become their* ANGEL *or* MAN/WOMAN *characters.*)

ANGEL 1: All right. Let's try this next house.

ANGEL 2: Yeah, and please try and be on key this time.

ANGEL 3: It's not my fault you start in too high a key.

ANGEL 2: OK. Here we are. 1, 2, 3, 4 . . .

ALL *(out of tune):* "Joy to the world, the Lord has come . . ."

MAN: Hey! Hey! Hey! Don't you know what time it is? It's a little late for caroling isn't it?

ANGELs: Merry Christmas!

MAN: Same to you . . . Hey! I don't recognize you. Who are you?

ANGEL 1: We're angels.

MAN: Cute! So, what are you? A basketball team?

ANGEL 2: No, we're angels.

MAN: OK. I see. You're like the scouts? Out doing good, huh? How cute.

ANGEL 3: No, we're angels.

MAN: All right. I give up. Whatever you are, I've got to get back and put together my child's Christmas present. How much do I need to contribute for that lovely song?

ANGEL 1: Owe? Nothing. At least not money.

MAN: Well . . . OK. Are you sure? I'm a generous guy, you know.

ANGEL 2: We're not doing it for the money.

MAN *(laughing):* Then why are you doing it?

ANGEL 3: To remind people what it was like on the day Jesus was born.

MAN: All right. I'll bite. What was it like?

ANGEL 3: Cold.

ANGEL 1: Actually, it was glorious. Thousands of angels filling the sky.

18

ANGEL 2: It was so bright you couldn't tell if it was midnight or noon. And singing, "Peace on earth, peace to men!" Announcing that our King, your Savior, was born.

ANGEL 3: The sound echoed through the hillsides. It's a pity the only ones who heard it were those poor shepherds. They were so terrified at first, they didn't know what to do.

ANGEL 1: Yeah. But once they stopped shaking, they ran . . . no they flew to the stable to see Jesus and worship Him.

MAN: Bravo. Great job. And you don't have a script to cheat off of or anything. I'm impressed. Now, I really must get going. I have this XJ Turbo Tank to build for my son's Christmas present.

ANGEL 1: We're talking about the birth of the King here. What's more important at Christmas than that?

MAN: Look, this tank isn't going to build itself. If it's not under the tree tomorrow morning, are you going to be the one to explain it to my sobbing son?

ANGEL 2: OK. We'll let you go, but let me ask you a question. What if we told you that the greatest president ever to live was born tonight?

MAN: I'd say you were crazy. You can't predict stuff like that.

ANGEL 3: Why not? We knew when Jesus was born.

MAN: Yeah. That was different. Jesus didn't have to run for office—it was handed to Him. It's hard work running for president. You gotta serve the public for a while, make a name for yourself, become popular, get some dirt on the other guy. You just can't predict someone being president.

ANGEL 3: Let's say we did, and told you about it. What would you do?

MAN: I don't know. What could I do?

ANGEL 1: Wouldn't you want to see for yourself?

MAN: Nah. I don't go for babies.

ANGEL 2: Wouldn't you want to tell your friends then?

MAN: Who would believe me? They'd lock me up. Saying I'd seen angels and knew the future—yup, I'd be locked up for years.

ANGEL 3: Perhaps you are right. People might think you were crazy. That didn't stop the shepherds . . . or the early disciples.

MAN: Yeah. Well, we don't need to invent stories like that anymore. I guess we've grown out of needing them.

ANGEL 1: Perhaps you have. Besides, why would anyone want to spread good news?

ANGEL 2 *(after long pause):* Merry Christmas, sir.

MAN: Sure. Merry Christmas to you too. Now, if you'll excuse me . . .

ANGEL 3: Right. The tank. We won't take up any more of your time.

(MAN *freezes.*)

ANGEL 2: Well, angels. Let's try the next house.

ANGELS *(out of tune):* "Joy to the world, the Lord has come . . ."

(Freeze)

I Can't Wait 'til Christmas
A Play in Two Acts
by Chuck Wood

Running Time: Act I—30 minutes; Act II—15 minutes

Synopsis: Nursing home resident Kate has developed over time a bitter negative attitude about life and people around her to the point that she has shut out just about everyone. Kate gets a new roommate, Rose, who allows God to use her in reaching out to Kate with Christian love. Rose's love and her living example begin to affect Kate's life in a new way. A former caregiver of Rose, a young woman named Rita, confirms to Kate that the love coming from Rose is genuine. Finally, just a few days before Christmas, the once-bitter Kate is touched so deeply by the new life she is experiencing that she is ready to take one of the most important steps in her lifetime.

Cast:
>KATE—A senior nursing home resident with an attitude problem
>ROSE—Kate's new roommate; a positive, loving, Christian lady
>RITA—A first-year college student who has been caring for Rose
>MAY—A nursing home employee (housekeeping), friend of Kate
>PAT—A nurse who is just about fed up with Kate's attitude
>DR. WRIGHT—A physician hired to make weekly visits to Harvest Home
>CHRISTMAS CAROLERS—Heard from offstage

Production Notes: In a nursing home room for two residents, there are two single beds. Kate's bed is on the left side of the stage, Rose's bed on the right side. Call buttons are located near the beds. Small end tables for water pitchers and glasses are placed at the ends of the beds. Also needed in the room are a wastebasket and a flowerpot of artificial flowers anchored in Styrofoam. There is a window to the left of the stage. The entrance may be centered or to the right (whichever is more convenient on your stage). Stage directions for this script are written for the entrance being centered. As space is available, there may be dressers and closets.

Act I

Setting: Harvest Home—a senior nursing facility

Time: Early December in a place where there is snow

(KATE is looking out the window. She continues to take in a winter scene beyond the window as MAY enters with a pitcher of water.)

MAY: Fresh water for you, Miss Kate.

KATE: Ice water in winter. Exactly what I need.

MAY: Just doing my job.

KATE: Snowing again.

MAY *(changing water pitchers):* Like you said, it's winter.

KATE: I enjoy watching the birds out there. Do you like to look at the birds?

MAY: I've seen them. Pigeons.

KATE: Doves.

MAY: If you say so.

KATE: Want to watch them with me?

MAY: Maybe later. I've got too much to do right now.

KATE *(turning from window, to MAY):* You don't have enough time, and time's all I've got.

MAY *(beginning to exit, turns to look back at KATE):* You've got a point there.

KATE: Day's pass so slow, May.

MAY: I might stop by on my break, if I get one.

KATE: That's OK. You don't have to.

MAY: I heard you're getting a roommate. Maybe good company is what you need.

KATE: That hasn't been my luck lately.

MAY: How's that?

KATE: After beginning to know them, they die. I'm tired of getting close.

22

MAY: Remember Miss Bess. You liked her, and she didn't die.

KATE: But she got better. And her daughter took her back home.

MAY: For a while, the company was good.

KATE: Nothing good lasts.

MAY: Sorry to rain on your parade.

KATE: I try not to be negative. But Harvest Home's not my cup of tea.

MAY: You think it's my cup of tea? Follow me around some day.

KATE: So you don't like being stuck with people like me.

MAY: I'm sorry I said that. There's just not enough of me to make everyone here at the nursing home happy, and then I go back to my house and try to do the same thing.

KATE: Thanks for the fresh water . . . and for the conversation. You didn't have to stay and talk, but you did.

MAY *(turning to exit):* I'll be back. *(Looking back)* It's a promise.

KATE: See you later.

(After MAY *leaves,* KATE *pours herself some ice water, takes a drink, and walks toward the window again.)*

KATE: Brrrrr.

PAT *(entering):* I heard that. Are you cold?

KATE: No.

PAT: But you went "brrrrr." I distinctly heard you.

KATE: The doves. Do you think they're cold?

PAT: I wouldn't know.

KATE: Feathers. You believe they're as warm as fur?

PAT: Don't ask me. I studied people in nursing school, not birds and animals.

KATE: I still think you'd have an opinion.

PAT *(handing* KATE *a small container of pills):* Time for your medicine, Kate.

KATE: I don't know why I have to take these pills. I'm not sick.

PAT: Maybe this medicine is what's keeping you well.

KATE: The pills are not about wellness. They're about money, and you know it.

PAT: That's not a good attitude.

KATE: See this pill. Costs a few cents to make. Distributor buys it for a cost of two dollars. Sells it to Harvest Home for ten dollars. Harvest Home makes me swallow it and charges Medicaid or Medicare twenty dollars. It's about money, Pat.

PAT: How do you know your figures are right?

KATE: I'm sure they're not completely right.

PAT: It's nice of you to admit it.

KATE: The true profit's probably even higher. I forgot to mention a lot of other people who take their cut.

PAT: Just swallow the pills.

KATE: What if I don't.

PAT: Swallow them.

(KATE *pretends to swallow the pills with her water. She takes a big drink but keeps the pills hidden in her hand.*)

PAT: That's a good girl, Kate. Now, I've got to check your heart and lungs.

(*As the conversation continues,* PAT *checks* KATE*'s heartbeat and breathing.*)

KATE (*sitting on her bed*): I heard I'm getting a new roommate.

PAT: She's being shown around the home now.

KATE: What do you know about her?

PAT: She's old.

KATE: Big deal. What else?

PAT: She needs some assistance.

KATE: Wow! Aren't you a big help.

PAT (*with stethoscope*): Shhh, while I check your heartbeat. (*Pause*) A little fast, but your medicine will take care of it. You'll have lots of time to get to know your new roommate.

KATE: What's her name?

PAT: I haven't seen her chart yet. Now your breathing. Shhhh. *(Pause)* Sounds OK.

KATE: Is her family with her?

PAT: A young lady brought her here.

KATE: Maybe her daughter.

PAT: I don't think so. I heard the young lady has been looking after the old woman, but she can't do it any longer.

KATE: Is that all you found out about her?

PAT: I'll leave that up to you to find out more.

KATE: My breathing is always OK. Why do you keep having to check it?

PAT: I'm just doing my job, Kate.

KATE: Wouldn't want to hold you back from earning a living.

PAT: Look, Kate, I don't know who stole your mistletoe. I don't know what grinch you've been keeping company with. Your attitude . . . well, I'm not going to say it, but the kids today have a word for it. You probably know what I mean.

KATE: That bad, huh.

PAT: Just don't spoil it for your new roommate.

KATE: Maybe you're right.

PAT: And don't spoil Christmas for yourself. I suppose you've got some reasons for your attitude, but get over it, Kate. *(Exiting)* Get over it!

KATE *(after a pause, she rises, then starts singing very quietly and slowly):* "Jingle bells, jingle bells, jingle all the way . . ." *(Moves to the doorway and loudly sings into the hall)* "Oh, what fun it is to ride in a one-horse open sleigh!" *(Shouting into the hall)* How's that for good Christmas spirit, Nurse Pat? How's that? *(Returns to the room, her fist becomes an open hand containing pills. One-by-one she takes them out of her hand.)* Pink pill. Blue pill. Purple pill. Big pill. Little pill. Square pill. Round pill. And I know just where you all belong.

(KATE moves the wastebasket from its partially hidden location to within audience view, faces audience, and throws the pills into the wastebasket, one-by-one. Then she picks up the basket and begins to return it to its previous location. While she still has the basket in hand, MAY opens the doorway.)

MAY: I saw that!

KATE: You did?

MAY: I did.

KATE: Saw everything?

MAY: What do you mean "everything?"

KATE: What do you *think* I mean?

MAY: I saw you move the wastebasket from its assigned place.

KATE: Is that *all* you saw?

MAY: Was there more I should have seen?

KATE: Don't ask *me? Was* there?

MAY: You've got a guilty look about you.

KATE: Now you're accusing me too. Picking on me. Like the others.

MAY: Picking on you? I may be the only true friend you've got around here.

KATE: You were accusing me. Don't deny it.

MAY: Accusing you of what?

KATE: Of having a guilty look. Which means you think I did something wrong, other than move the wastebasket.

MAY: I'm sorry.

KATE: Apology accepted.

MAY: Could you give me the basket. I need to empty it.

KATE: Nothing in it.

MAY: There's always something in it.

KATE: Wait 'til later. 'Til it's full. Come back then. It'll still be here.

MAY: You're right. Just put the wastebasket back where it belongs. I'll get it later.

KATE: You probably have other things to do anyway.

MAY: Come to think of it, I do. But I don't remember what.

KATE: What were you doing before you came into my room?

MAY: Can't recall.

KATE: Why did you come in here?

MAY: Can't remember that either.

KATE: You did tell me you'd be back to visit me. Maybe you were just making good on your promise.

MAY: Who knows? *(Lightbulb moment!)* Now I remember!

KATE: OK, let's have it.

MAY: I wanted to tell you that your new roommate is in the building.

KATE: Nurse Pat already told me.

MAY: Well, got to go. Sorry about the accusation. I was out of line.

KATE: That's OK.

MAY *(leaving):* See you.

(After MAY leaves, KATE picks the pills out of the wastebasket.)

KATE: Square pill. Round pill. Little pill. Big pill. Purple pill. Blue pill. Pink pill. I believe I've got them all. Was there a green pill? Don't think so.

(KATE lifts an artificial flower from its pot, drops the pills into the pot, and puts the flowers back. At this point, NURSE PAT enters with ROSE, the new roommate. ROSE uses a cane to help her get around. ROSE walks stage right, looks around, stops in front of the bed. Accompanying ROSE is RITA, a young lady who had been living with ROSE and caring for her. RITA is carrying two suitcases.)

PAT: Rose, this is your new home. You will be sharing this room with Kate.

KATE: That's me.

ROSE: Kate. That's a pretty name. This is Rita. She has been living with me and taking care of me, but she can't do it any longer.

RITA: Nice to meet you, Miss . . . Mrs . . .

KATE: It's OK if you call me Kate.

ROSE: Go ahead, Rita. She said it would be all right.

27

RITA: I'm not comfortable calling adults by their first name.

KATE: OK, how about "Miss Kate?"

RITA: I guess I could be comfortable with that.

PAT: I'll get Rose settled in, Rita. Just put those suitcases down for now. Could you go to your car and bring in anything else you brought?

ROSE: Thank you, Rita.

RITA *(exiting):* I'll be right back.

ROSE: She's such a good girl. Don't know what I'd do without her. But now I'm about to find out.

PAT: You'll be in good hands at Harvest Home.

ROSE *(sitting on her bed at right):* Harvest Home . . . Has a nice sound. Good name.

KATE: Ever wonder why they call it that?

PAT: That's enough, Kate.

KATE: There's a lot in a name. Think about it for a moment. Harvest Home. What does that tell you, Rose?

ROSE: I never thought about it.

KATE: I'll bet you're thinking about it now.

PAT: Enough, Kate!

KATE *(sits on her bed at left):* Nurse Pat thinks I have a negative attitude.

PAT: Pretend you're not hearing this, Rose.

ROSE: Don't have to pretend anything.

PAT: I don't follow you.

ROSE: All I have to do is think about something else.

PAT: In that case, I believe you'll be able to get along with Kate.

KATE: I'm not hard to get along with. You just have to understand where I'm coming from.

ROSE: We'll do just fine.

KATE: See, Pat, Rose is exactly what I need.

PAT: But are *you* what *she* needs?

KATE: You put her in here with me.

PAT: I had nothing to do with it. Administrative decision all the way.

KATE: From what I've heard, this is the only bed open. You didn't have much choice, Rose.

ROSE: This room is OK with me.

PAT: Don't ruin it for her, Kate.

ROSE: Nurse Pat?

PAT: Yes.

ROSE: I was told not to bring my medicine. That Harvest Home would furnish the pills.

PAT: You were told right.

KATE: Let me tell you a bit about that.

PAT: Kate, why don't you go to the dining hall and find out what's for dinner. I'm sure Rose would like to know what she'll be eating this evening.

KATE: Like she has a choice.

PAT: Just go.

KATE: Trying to get rid of me.

PAT: I'm giving you an opportunity to show Rose how nice you can be.

ROSE: Thank you, Kate. I think I'd like to know what's for dinner.

KATE *(rising):* Since you asked me, I guess I don't mind.

PAT: Bye, Kate.

KATE *(exiting):* I'll be back soon, Rose.

ROSE: You made a comment a moment ago. You told Kate not to ruin it for me. What did you mean by that?

PAT *(sits on* KATE*'s bed):* Some people have trouble getting along with Kate.

ROSE: Some people have trouble getting along with anyone.

PAT: Most people have trouble getting along with Kate.

29

ROSE: I'm not most people. We'll be just fine together.

PAT: I hope so.

ROSE: About the medicine.

PAT: We'll make sure you get what the doctor prescribed. And when you are scheduled to take it.

ROSE: I'm not sure I need all the pills I'm supposed to take each day, but I know the blue pill is very necessary. Don't forget the blue pill. It's funny-shaped. And has this design on it.

PAT: I think I know which one you mean. Kate takes it too. You miss taking that one, and you're in trouble. Especially if you get too excited.

ROSE: That bad, huh?

PAT *(rises):* If it's the one I'm thinking about.

ROSE: You sound like you know what you're doing.

PAT: I'm a nurse, Rose.

ROSE: Don't mean to sound offensive, Nurse Pat. I didn't mean it that way at all.

PAT: Then I won't take it that way.

(RITA enters with another suitcase . . . a smaller one than the other two.)

RITA: I think this is all. We really didn't bring too much. Are you sure you have enough?

ROSE: I won't be going anywhere. I brought all I'll need.

PAT: We have the number to call if she needs to have anything else.

RITA: I'll be gone a lot, but there's an answering machine.

ROSE: Rita will be going to Community College. And working part-time. Busy girl.

PAT: Speaking of busy, I have some other patients to check on. Nice to meet you, Rita. *(Walking toward door, looks back)* I'll check on you later, Rose.

RITA: Are we doing the right thing, Rose . . . putting you in here?

ROSE: Don't include yourself with the "we." Family put me here. If it hadn't been for you, I would have been in here long ago.

RITA: It just seemed right to help care for you. When the church told me about your need, I couldn't have done anything else.

ROSE: You've taken good care of me, Rita.

RITA: And you've given me a place to stay. Don't forget that.

ROSE: Small price for your care and your company. Bring me that small suitcase.

RITA *(bringing her the suitcase):* Where should I put it?

ROSE: Right here on the bed. Now open it.

RITA: Wow! Some pretty interesting stuff.

ROSE: Special mementos. All to remind me of special times and special people. I just want to have them with me. This is the first Valentine's card my late husband, Al, gave me.

RITA: You loved him. I can tell.

ROSE: I loved nobody else. No other man, that is.

RITA: I wish I could have known him.

ROSE: This is the last Mother's Day card my daughter, Jane, sent me.

RITA: I see where she signed her name. Only her name. I would think she could have written, "Love, Jane."

ROSE: At least I got a card from her. The others felt that a phone call on Mother's Day was enough. But you can't save a phone call like you can save a card or letter.

RITA: I'll stop by, and I'll write to you. And I promise you the best Christmas card ever.

ROSE: Child, you're a gift from God.

RITA: Is there something you'd like me to get you for Christmas?

ROSE: Just you. Stop by when you can. And when you can't, keep praying for me.

RITA: You can count on that.

ROSE: I love you, Rita.

RITA *(reaching out to hug* ROSE*):* And I love you.

KATE *(entering quickly):* You'll never believe what we're having for dinner. *(Stops suddenly)* Sorry. Am I interrupting anything?

ROSE: We're saying our good-byes.

KATE: Maybe I should leave you two alone.

RITA *(standing):* I was just leaving, Miss Kate.

KATE: The hug. It's good to see that.

ROSE: Rita and I do that a lot.

KATE: And saying, "I love you." I don't hear that very often.

ROSE: Well, maybe you should.

RITA: We have this special "love" thing we say to each other every day.

ROSE: Maybe Kate doesn't want to hear it.

KATE: You've got me curious.

RITA: OK, here goes. Jesus loves you.

ROSE: And I do too.

*(*KATE *does not respond—she says nothing.)*

ROSE: Well?

KATE: Well, what?

ROSE: Your reaction?

KATE: Do I have to react?

RITA: Jesus loves you, Miss Kate.

ROSE: And we do too!

KATE *(walking stage left):* Nobody loves me.

ROSE: Don't you believe us?

KATE *(looking down):* You haven't been around me. You don't know me.

RITA: But Jesus does.

ROSE: And if He loves you, how can we not love you.

KATE *(uncomfortable, changing the subject, looks at them):* About dinner . . .

ROSE: What about dinner?

KATE: They're having steak!

ROSE: So?

KATE: You know how long it's been since they served steak?

RITA: Why don't I leave now so you two can talk about dinner.

KATE: No need to rush.

RITA: I was about ready to leave when you walked in. *(Walking toward door)* I'll try to stop by on Sunday.

ROSE: I'll be waiting. And thanks so much, Rita.

RITA *(exiting):* Love you.

KATE: I believe she really does.

ROSE: I *know* she does.

KATE: You hear those words, but it's not often that you see love.

ROSE: And Rita is not even family. Family has to love you.

KATE: Has to?

ROSE: You're right. Nobody can be forced to love.

KATE *(sits on her bed):* I think I'm going to like you, Rose.

ROSE: We'll get along just fine.

KATE: Almost dinnertime.

ROSE: We'll talk more at the dinner table.

KATE: The two of us won't be eating at the same table.

ROSE: Why not?

KATE: When you have to sit with nonroommates, you get to know more people. At least, that's Harvest Home's philosophy.

ROSE: I suppose that makes sense.

KATE: I don't like the people I sit with. *(Standing, showing a rise in frustration)* Sometimes they make me so mad.

ROSE: Why?

KATE: Lots of things. Bad manners mostly. Doing things you're not supposed to see and making sounds you're not supposed to hear at the table. You want to hear some examples?

33

ROSE: I'll just leave it to my imagination.

KATE: You really don't want to hear?

ROSE: I'd like to be able to eat my dinner.

KATE *(sitting again):* This evening, I'll just put cotton in my ears, close my eyes . . . shut out everything around me, and enjoy my steak.

ROSE: Steak sounds nice.

KATE: It's rare that they serve steak.

ROSE: Really?

KATE: You didn't get it, did you?

ROSE: Get what?

KATE: Rare . . . steak . . . an attempt at humor.

ROSE: Ha . . . ha . . . ha . . .

KATE: *Fake* laugh.

ROSE: That's not nice to say.

KATE: Remember, I'm not nice. *(A little upset)*

ROSE: It was funny. Really.

KATE: You're just saying that to be nice.

ROSE: Sometimes "being nice" is the way to go.

KATE: Are you saying that I'm not nice?

ROSE: You're the one who said that you're not nice.

KATE: This place will make you that way. Adjusting to life here is a bitter pill to swallow.

ROSE: Speaking of pills. I normally take some of mine before dinner.

KATE: Hit your call button. They'll come around.

ROSE: Maybe I should wait. I've still got a few minutes.

KATE *(still upset):* If you want help later, hit the call button now. It'll be later when they finally get here.

ROSE *(hitting the call button):* I suppose so.

KATE: You need those pills. I still can't believe we're going to eat steak.

ROSE: I like mine medium-rare.

KATE: You'll take it however they serve it . . . and be glad you get any at all.

ROSE: I guess that calls for smiling anyway, praising the Lord, and having a good attitude.

KATE: A good attitude doesn't come easy in this place.

ROSE: Are you having some attitude problems right now?

KATE *(standing):* So you're picking on me too.

ROSE: I'm not picking.

KATE *(more upset):* Don't I have a right to express myself?

ROSE: Calm down, Kate. Being upset is not good for you.

KATE *(really upset):* You know what's not good for me? Everything?

ROSE: Surely not everything.

KATE *(intense):* Take the food. Sure, we have steak tonight. But what about the other days? Beans and greens . . . beans and franks . . . leathery macaroni and cheese . . . peas and cabbage. *(Uncomfortable silence)* Oh, my!

ROSE: What is it?

KATE: I don't feel so good.

ROSE: You want to hear how long since I have felt good?

KATE: This is different.

ROSE: In what way?

KATE: I don't like how I feel right now.

ROSE: Who does? We just have to go on and make the best of it.

KATE: This is no joke, Rose.

ROSE: Do you think you're going to be sick?

KATE: I think I'm already sick.

ROSE: Maybe you should lie down.

KATE (lying down): It's hot in here.

ROSE: The temperature is OK, Kate. Very comfortable.

KATE: And it's hard to breathe.

ROSE: I'll hit the call button for the nurse.

KATE: The call button is already on. Remember?

ROSE: What can I do?

KATE: The flowerpot.

ROSE: Flowers at a time like this?

KATE: Please! The flower pot.

ROSE (aside): She's delusional.

KATE: The blue one. Bring me the blue one!

ROSE: There are no blue ones

KATE: The funny-shaped blue one . . . with the design on it.

ROSE: Sorry, Kate, but you're seeing things that aren't there. (Going to the door) Nurse! Nurse!

KATE: Tell them to hurry.

ROSE: In here! Kate's sick. Bad, I think.

MAY (rushing in): What's wrong?

ROSE: Kate's not doing well.

MAY: She was OK about fifteen minutes ago.

ROSE: Well, she's not now.

MAY: Maybe I'd better look for Pat.

ROSE (going to KATE's bedside): The nurse will be here soon.

KATE: I feel sleepy, Rose.

ROSE: Try to stay awake 'til a nurse gets here.

KATE: I don't think I can.

ROSE: Yes, you can. Try hard.

KATE: Good night, Rose.

ROSE: Kate . . . Kate . . . Say something! *(A sudden change in* ROSE'*s mood)* My Jesus, help her. *(*ROSE *begins to pray.)* My dear God in heaven, help my friend Kate. Whatever is wrong, make it right. Touch her body, Lord. Send Your healing spirit.

PAT *(entering):* OK, what's up, Kate? I've got better things to do. *(To* ROSE.*)* Probably faking it again to get attention.

ROSE: I don't think so.

PAT: She's sleeping. At least she won't bother us for awhile.

ROSE: She went to sleep too fast. This doesn't look good.

PAT: I don't understand. I gave her all her medication just before you checked in.

ROSE: Do something. She needs help.

PAT: Did you notice anything different before she got sick?

ROSE: Well, she did get pretty upset.

PAT: She takes medicine for controlling her anger.

ROSE: She got very excited. Really fast. I tried to calm her down. No use.

PAT *(going to* KATE'*s side, trying to shake her awake):* Kate! You can open your eyes now, Kate. You don't want to miss dinner.

ROSE: She was looking forward to steak.

PAT *(mood changing to a serious one):* I don't think she's faking. Maybe I'd better call the emergency squad. *(Leaving hurriedly)*

ROSE *(going to* KATE'*s bedside again):* If you can hear me, Kate, move your hand . . . blink your eyes . . . do anything. *(Lights being to fade.* ROSE *begins to pray again.)* Jesus, touch her. Send Your healing into this room. She's my friend. Keep Kate with us. Hear my prayer.

*(*ROSE *continues to be in a prayerful mode as the lights fade out completely.)*

Act II

Setting: Harvest Home

Time: Three days before Christmas

(Lights come up revealing KATE *sitting on her bed. Near her is* DR. WRIGHT. *He stops by once a week to touch base with patients who have recently had health problems.* ROSE *is out of the room, in the dining hall for a religious service. It is now just a few days before Christmas. Some added decorations and a little Christmas tree brighten the room.)*

DR. WRIGHT: Hold your arms out. (KATE *does.)* Now bring your hands together. (KATE *does.)* Touch your nose.

KATE: Aren't you going to look down my throat?

DR. WRIGHT: You've been having coordination problems. Not a sore throat.

KATE: Maybe you can hit my knee with a hammer.

DR. WRIGHT: Let me do this my way, Kate.

KATE: Look. I'm OK now. I have been for a couple of weeks.

DR. WRIGHT: I just want to make sure you've recovered.

KATE: I'm OK. Trust me.

DR. WRIGHT: You're lucky you had a roommate when you passed out. If you had been alone, it could have been more serious.

KATE: Rose doesn't think it was luck that she was here.

DR. WRIGHT: Providence, huh?

KATE: She called it God's will.

DR. WRIGHT: Maybe it was. Anyway, I think you'll be in good health to enjoy Christmas.

KATE: Thanks for looking in on me, Doctor.

DR. WRIGHT: You've changed.

KATE: A little older, but that happens to everybody.

DR. WRIGHT: No. A little nicer.

KATE: You really think so?

DR. WRIGHT: You seem more relaxed.

KATE: Could be the medication.

DR. WRIGHT: Nurse Pat says it's been a while since you got mad . . . threw a fit.

KATE: Nurse Pat said something nice about me?

DR. WRIGHT: Said you haven't been complaining as much.

KATE: I guess things are starting to get better. What else can I say?

DR. WRIGHT: Well, I have to finish my rounds.

KATE: Merry Christmas, Dr. Wright.

DR. WRIGHT: And Merry Christmas to you, Kate.

KATE: Give my best to your family.

DR. WRIGHT: I'll do that. See you next year.

KATE: That's a long time. What if I get sick in the next couple of weeks?

DR. WRIGHT: In a couple of weeks, it will be next year.

KATE: Oh, yeah. That's right, Dr. Wright.

DR. WRIGHT: Trying to be funny.

KATE: Well, wasn't it?

DR. WRIGHT: Sure. *(Chuckles)*

KATE: See you next year.

DR. WRIGHT: Right!

KATE: I'm sure Rose wishes you well. She's in the dining hall. Attending a religious service.

DR. WRIGHT *(exiting):* Give her my best.

(MAY enters. She is in a happy mood as she goes to the wastebasket, picks it up, and heads for the doorway.)

MAY: How are things today, Kate?

KATE: It's a good day, May.

MAY *(from the hallway outside the door):* Been watching the pigeons today?

KATE: Doves.

MAY *(re-entering with wastebasket, returning it to its location):* Same thing.

KATE: Ever hear of a pigeon being the symbol of peace?

39

MAY: What's that got to do with it?

KATE: Rose told me about how Jesus is the Prince of Peace. And how natural it is for us to see doves, another symbol of peace, just outside the window at Christmastime.

MAY: I've noticed that you've opened up to Rose more than any other person.

KATE: She's been the best thing that has happened to me.

MAY: Do you want any fresh water?

KATE: Not now.

MAY: Maybe I'd better look at that flower. Seems to be wilting.

KATE: It's artificial, and you know it.

MAY: I never told anybody your secret about the hidden pills.

KATE: How did you know?

MAY: Found them by accident while I was cleaning.

KATE: I won't do it again. I promise.

MAY *(starting to leave):* Well, there's more work to do. Good to see you doing OK.

(As MAY exits, ROSE enters. She is in a happy mood.)

ROSE: What a good time we had in the dining hall. We sang so many Christmas carols. Everybody got to pick their favorite, and then we all sang together. You should have been there.

KATE *(still sitting on her bed):* I had to stay in here for the doctor's visit.

ROSE: What did the doctor say?

KATE: Said I am doing OK.

ROSE: Thank You, Jesus.

KATE: The doctor also said you had a lot to do with it.

ROSE: Maybe so. But if I did, it was only the Lord using me.

KATE: We're supposed to have a big Christmas party in the dining hall this evening.

ROSE: I heard. Presents and goodies. Makes me feel like a kid again.

KATE: Carolers are also supposed to come today and entertain us.

ROSE: Are you going to the party?

KATE: Wouldn't miss it.

ROSE: Was last year's party a good one?

KATE: Don't know.

ROSE: You can't remember?

KATE: Didn't go.

ROSE: Well, what about the year before that?

KATE: Didn't go.

ROSE: It does my heart good that you're going this year.

KATE: All because of you, Rose.

(NURSE PAT enters, smiling, holding two little cups of pills.)

PAT: Medicine time, girls. Open wide. *(Handing cup of pills to ROSE.)* Just two, Rose. Here they are. *(ROSE takes the pills, pours some water in her glass, and takes the pills. PAT hands KATE her pills.)* Still a cupfull, Kate. But the doctor says you have to have them.

KATE *(taking cup, reaches for her glass and prepares to take the pills)*: Can't forget the blue one. All down the hatch. *(Swallows them)*

PAT: Good girl, Kate. And you too, Rose. Well, I have to finish my rounds.

KATE: Merry Christmas, Pat.

PAT: Merry Christmas to you too. Oh, I heard the carolers will be here soon.

KATE: I want to hear them. Will I see you at the party later?

PAT: With my Santa costume on.

KATE: I won't be in costume. Threw my grinch costume away.

ROSE: Merry Christmas, Pat. *(Sits on her bed)* And the Lord's blessings be upon you.

PAT: And you too, Rose. Thanks for what you've done for Kate. This is a Christmas to remember. (PAT *exits.*)

KATE: This is a Christmas to remember, Rose.

ROSE: Want to make it even more of a memory?

KATE *(standing):* In what way?

ROSE: You say that being around me has changed you.

KATE: It has. *(Walking stage left to* ROSE*)* I've never known anyone with as much love as you. *(Sitting on* ROSE'*s bed, alongside her.)*

ROSE: I do love you, Kate.

KATE: And you never put me down. Never did things to get me upset. You have listened to me like you really care.

ROSE: I do care.

KATE: You've got something special, Rose. Something I haven't known before.

ROSE: You can have it too.

KATE: I think I know what you mean. It's about Jesus, isn't it?

ROSE: He's not only the reason for the season, but the reason for all we do, and think, and feel.

KATE: How do you get all that He is inside of you?

ROSE: By believing, and trusting. By turning your back on the past. And inviting Him into your heart, and mind, and whole being.

KATE: Sound too easy. It can't be that easy.

(Suddenly RITA *enters, carrying a Christmas bag with two presents.)*

RITA: Surprise!

ROSE: Why, Rita! I didn't expect to see you today.

RITA: I just couldn't wait 'til Christmas. *(Takes two presents from the bag. To* ROSE.*)* For you, Miss Rose. For all you've done for me.

ROSE: I love you so much, child!

RITA *(to* KATE*):* And for you, Miss Kate. For all you've done for Miss Rose.

KATE *(accepting the gift):* I don't know what to say . . . except, "Thank you."

RITA: That's all you need to say.

KATE: I never did anything for Rose. She's the one who did everything for me.

RITA: Miss Rose needs to give. And you were there to receive her love. She has been that way to me too. I came to live with her, hoping I could show her love. But she gave me so much more than I could ever give her. Can you understand that?

KATE: I never knew a person who was so giving and so loving. Now I know why she's that way. Rose was explaining it to me when you walked in.

RITA: There's more of Jesus in Miss Rose than in anyone I've ever met.

ROSE: Such nice wrapping you chose for the presents, Rita.

RITA: Why don't you open them now?

ROSE: I've always had a thing about not opening presents until Christmas.

RITA: But I'm so anxious to see the look on your faces when you open them.

ROSE: You're stopping by on Christmas Day, aren't you?

RITA: Of course.

ROSE: Well, we could put the presents under our little tree and open them when you stop by on Christmas. What do you think, Kate?

KATE: Wait 'til Christmas?

ROSE: You can open yours now if you want. Don't let my tradition keep you from seeing what's inside the wrapping.

KATE: You mentioned wanting to see the look on our faces, Rita. In some ways, it doesn't really matter what's inside. Or when I find out. I hope the look on my face says, "Thanks for just thinking enough of me to bring me a gift." Your thoughtfulness and your caring mean everything. In that way, you're a lot like Rose.

RITA: Miss Rose rubs off on people that way. Just wait 'til you see yourself a few months down the road.

KATE: I can only imagine.

(Outside the window, we hear the CHRISTMAS CAROLERS. For dramatic effect, it would be better to have a few carolers singing well than lots of carolers singing loudly. As the CAROLERS sing, RITA, ROSE, and KATE pause to listen. The CAROLERS sing for only about a minute, then hum in harmony a quiet, beautiful carol they have chosen. The pace of the following conversation is slow. No rushing.)

KATE: Just think. The carolers came here to sing just because of us.

RITA: They didn't have to, but they did.

ROSE: That's what Jesus did. He came here just because of us.

RITA: And He didn't have to, but He did.

ROSE: That's what makes it so special.

KATE: Rose . . .

ROSE: Yes, Kate.

KATE: I was thinking of waiting until Christmas to invite Jesus into my heart.

RITA: Christmas is such a special time.

KATE: But I'm not sure I can wait 'til Christmas.

ROSE: Then don't wait.

KATE: How do I do it?

ROSE: Just ask Him to come in.

RITA: Not to visit, but to stay.

ROSE: Say good-bye to all that's behind you.

KATE: I'm ready.

RITA: We'll pray with you.

(ROSE, RITA, and KATE all bow their heads in silent prayer as the CAROLERS sing with reverence one verse of a special carol—or perhaps something like, "Into my heart, into my heart. Come into my heart, Lord Jesus." The main goal of the CAROLERS is not to "perform," but to provide the background mood to make KATE's moment of decision for Christ an impacting one.

Near the end of the carol, lights begin to dim. By the time the carol is finished, all stage lights will be off except enough lighting to provide a silhouette of KATE, ROSE, and RITA in prayer. After a couple of seconds, there is a blackout.)